PASCAL ★ BLANCHET

White Rapids

DRAWN & QUA

Translated by Helge Dascher.

FRENCH TO ENGLISH

Drawn & Quarterly
Post Office Box 48056
Montreal, Quebec
Canada H2V 4S8
www.drawnandquarterly.com

First Drawn & Quarterly edition: September 2007.
Printed in Canada.

Library and Archives Canada Cataloguing in Publication
ISBN 978-1-897299-24-1
Blanchet, Pascal, 1980-
White Rapids / Pascal Blanchet.
Translation of: Rapide blanc (Originally published in French by Les Éditions de la Pasteque, Montreal, 2006).
1. Rapide-Blanc (Québec)–History–Fiction. 2. Shawinigan Water and Power Company–History–Fiction. 3. Company towns–Québec (Province)–Rapide-Blanc–History–Fiction. I. Title.
NC1449.B47R3613 2007 741.5'971 C2007-901247-7

Drawn & Quarterly acknowledges the financial contribution of the Government of Canada through the Book Publishing Industry Development Program (BPIDP) and the Canada Council for the Arts for our publishing activities and for support of this edition.

Distributed in the USA by:
Farrar, Straus and Giroux
19 Union Square West
New York, NY 10003
Orders: 888.330.8477

Distributed in Canada by:
Raincoast Books
9050 Shaughnessy Street
Vancouver, BC V6P 6E5
Orders: 800.663.5714

White
Rapids
To my Father

In
Montreal,

That night,
Decisions
were being made.

507

SHAWINIGAN WATER & POWER COMPANY

205 .... ANOTHER

801 .... QUIET EVENING

AT 507 PLACE D'ARMES.

100 .... THE WATCHMAN

IS MAKING

HIS ROUNDS

& THE OFFICES

1200 .... ARE

ALL EMPTY.

ALL EXCEPT ONE...

LC A BOARD MEETING

IS STILL UNDERWAY

3409 UPSTAIRS.

THERE IS

IMPORTANT BUSINESS

TO BE SETTLED

TONIGHT.

Some twenty stories above

THE BOARD MEMBERS ARE WAITING ...

Shawinigan Water & Power Company

Founded in 1898, the company set up its first plant on the banks of the St. Maurice River by Shawinigan Falls, just north of Three Rivers.

There, the SW&P Co. developed hydroelectric power. Over the next 30 years, Shawinigan grew to become one of Quebec's largest industrial centers.

In the early decades of the twentieth century, the company built several other hydroelectric dams.

But the most ambitious project of all was presented to the company's president and shareholders in the late 1920s.

It was on the top floors of the Montreal headquarters where J. E. Aldred presented his verdict…

TO SERVE
THE
PEOPLE

VERDICT:

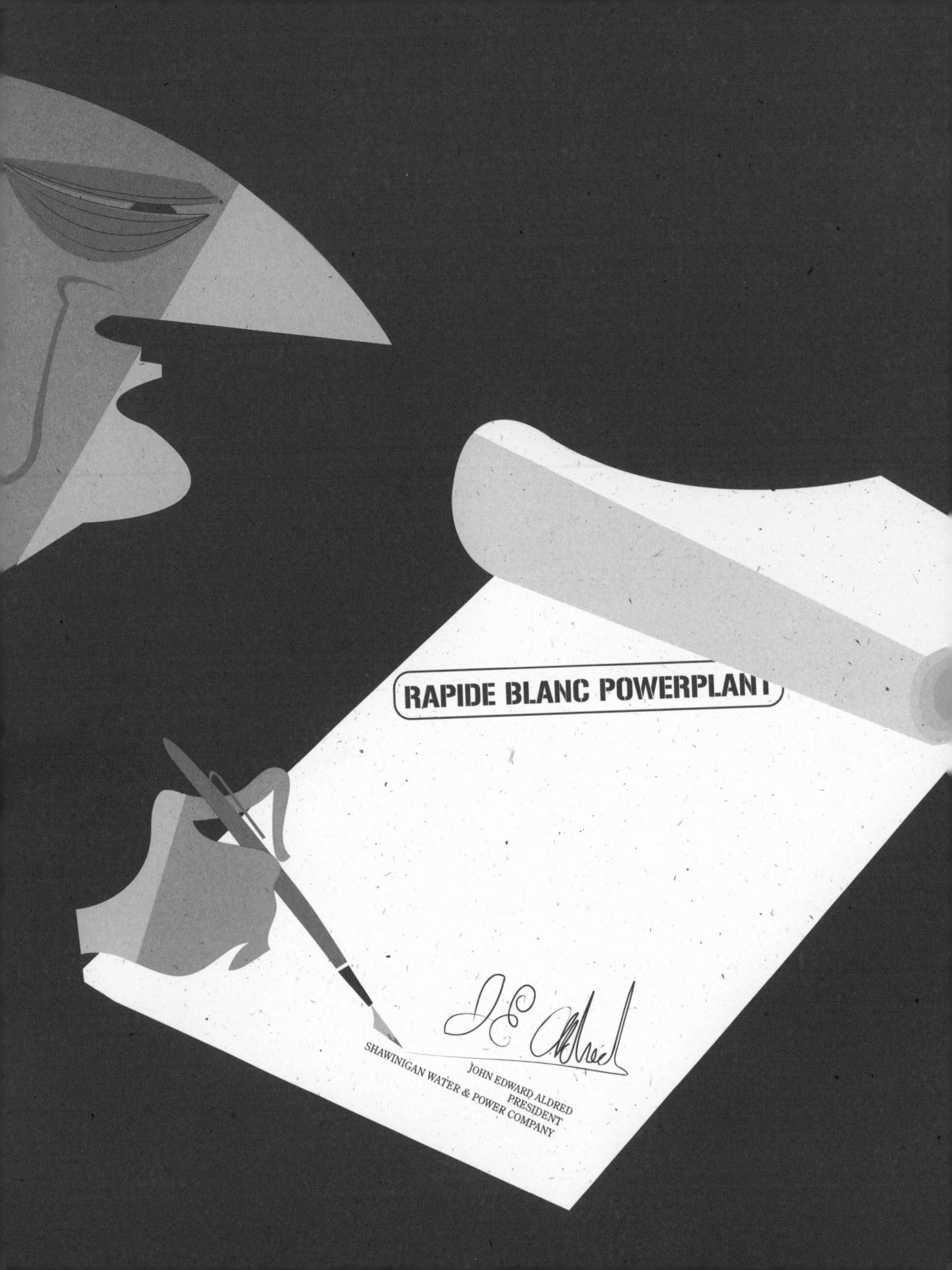
RAPIDE BLANC POWERPLANT
JOHN EDWARD ALDRED
PRESIDENT
SHAWINIGAN WATER & POWER COMPANY

On that cold December night, the story of Rapide Blanc, named after the white rapids running through a northern stretch of the St. Maurice River, was about to begin...

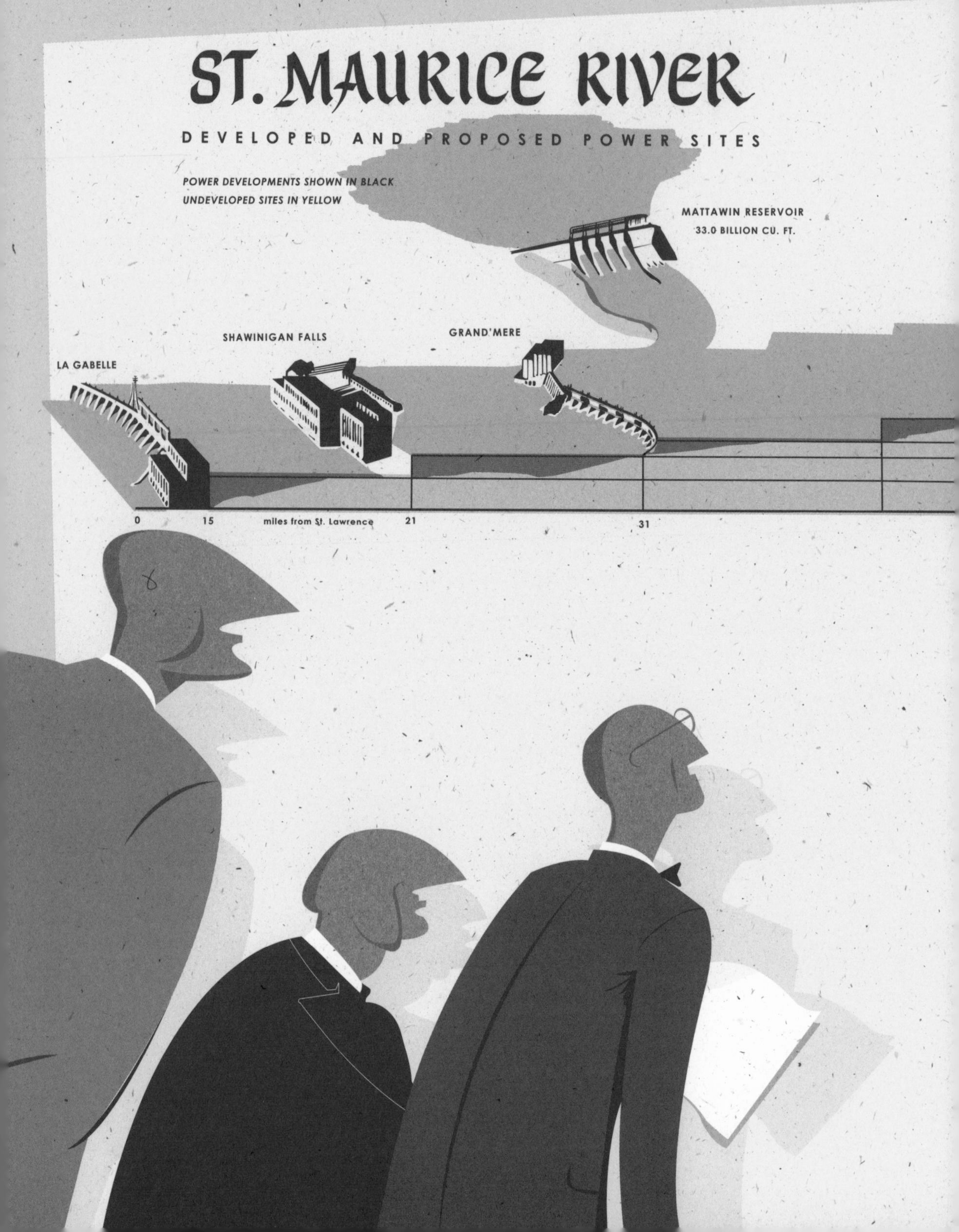
ST. MAURICE RIVER
DEVELOPED AND PROPOSED POWER SITES
POWER DEVELOPMENTS SHOWN IN BLACK
UNDEVELOPED SITES IN YELLOW
MATTAWIN RESERVOIR
33.0 BILLION CU. FT.
SHAWINIGAN FALLS
GRAND'MERE
LA GABELLE
0
15
miles from St. Lawrence
21
31

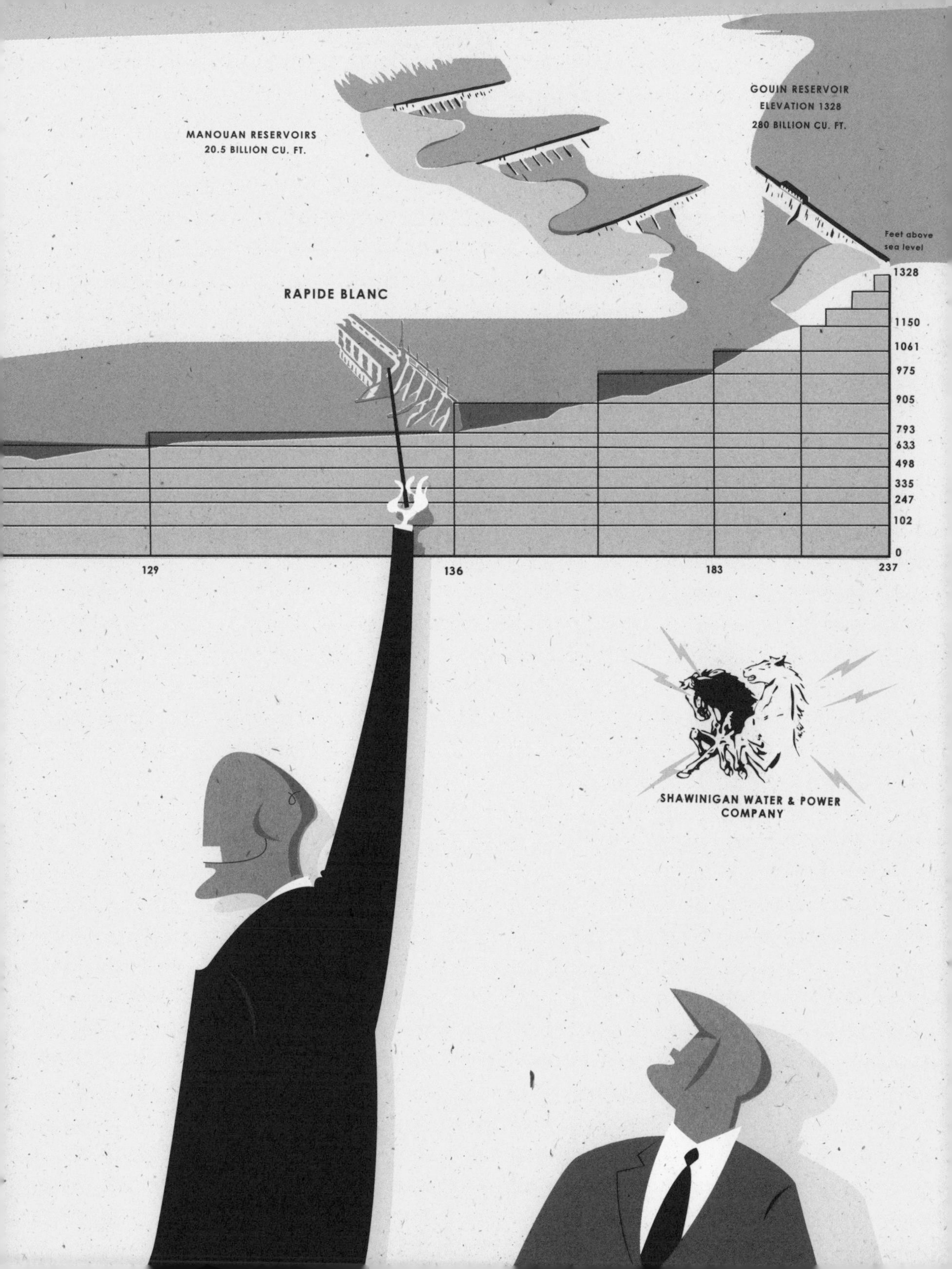
GOUIN RESERVOIR
ELEVATION 1328
280 BILLION CU. FT.
MANOUAN RESERVOIRS
20.5 BILLION CU. FT.
Feet above sea level
RAPIDE BLANC
1328
1150
1061
975
905
793
633
498
335
247
102
0
129
136
183
237
SHAWINIGAN WATER & POWER COMPANY

GOUIN RESERVOIR
GOUIN DAM
RAPIDE BLANC
ST. MAURICE RIVER
QUEBEC
GRANDMERE
SHAWINIGAN FALLS
SHAWINIGAN
LA GABELLE
THREE RIVERS
ST. LAWRENCE RIVER
MONTREAL

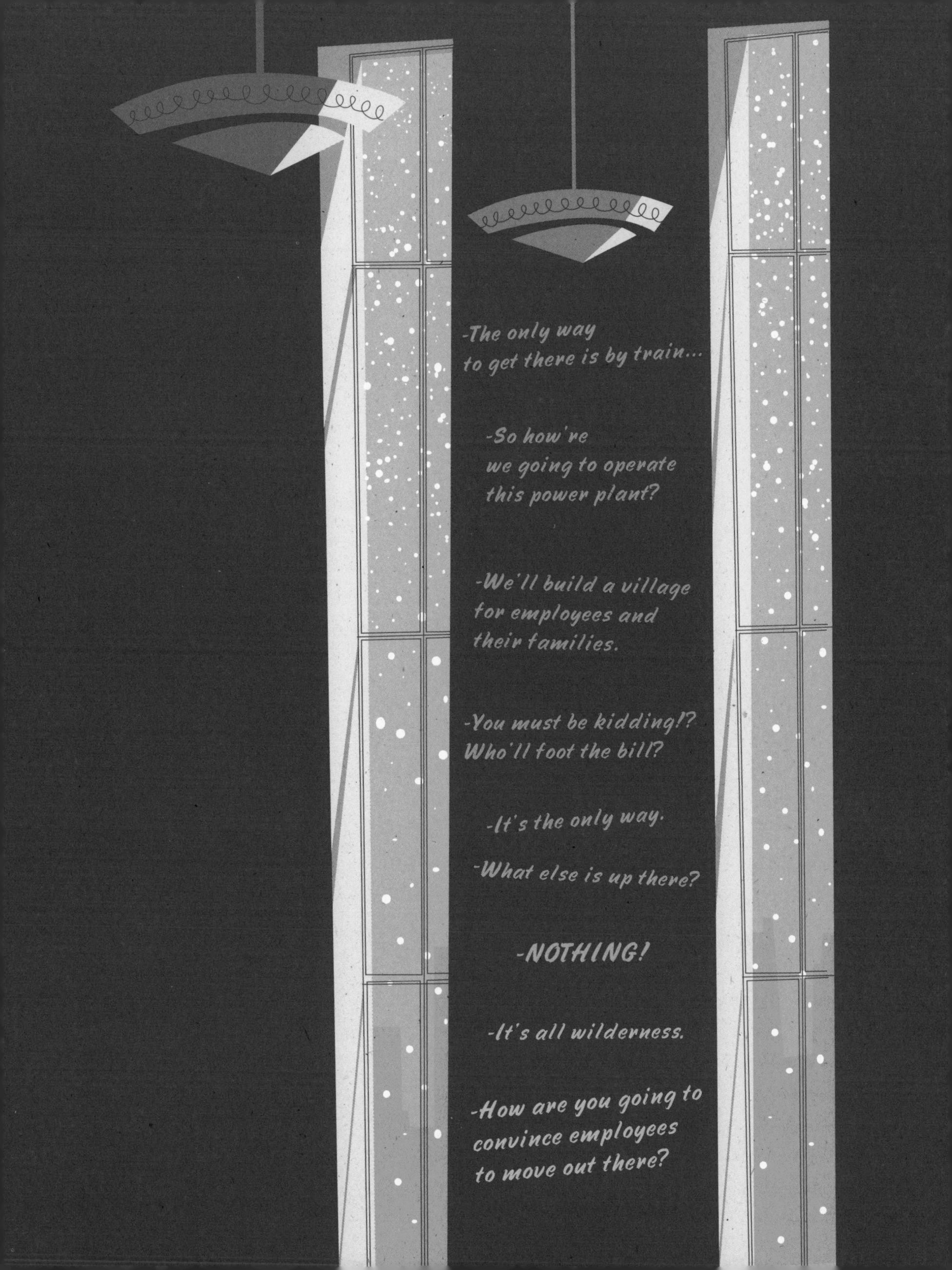
-The only way to get there is by train...
-So how're we going to operate this power plant?
-We'll build a village for employees and their families.
-You must be kidding!? Who'll foot the bill?
-It's the only way.
-What else is up there?
-NOTHING!
-It's all wilderness.
-How are you going to convince employees to move out there?

MANAGEMENT
ARCHITECTURE DEPARTMENT

I want a village! Plans, sections & elevations for tomorrow 8 am sharp!

Night passed...

Down by the Port, the Clock tower was about to Strike 8...

KNOCK-
KNOCK-
KNOCK-

Sir?

The architects presented
an elegant little town,
on par with Montreal's most stylish
neighborhoods. After all,
the company needed an incentive to
get employees to live out in
the middle of nowhere...

RAPIDE BLANC'S HOUSES

TWO FAMILY HOUSE

All Aboard!

SHAWINIGAN

LUMBERJACKS, EMPLOYEES AND FUTURE RESIDENTS OF RAPIDE BLANC: THEY ALL PASSED THROUGH THIS RAILROAD STATION.

WITH NO ROAD CONNECTING RAPIDE BLANC TO THE REST OF THE WORLD, MEN AND MATERIALS TRAVELED BY TRAIN. IT TOOK SIX YEARS AND MORE THAN 1000 MEN TO BUILD THE DAM AND POWER PLANT.

Northward
Bound

1934

INAUGURATION OF THE RAPIDE BLANC POWER PLANT AND DAM

Early on, workers and their families lived in camps, eager to see their new homes go up

BIT BY BIT, THE VILLAGE
THAT WOULD BE RAPIDE BLANC TOOK SHAPE.
STATELY BRICK HOUSES SOON LINED
CHIC CRESCENT STREET...

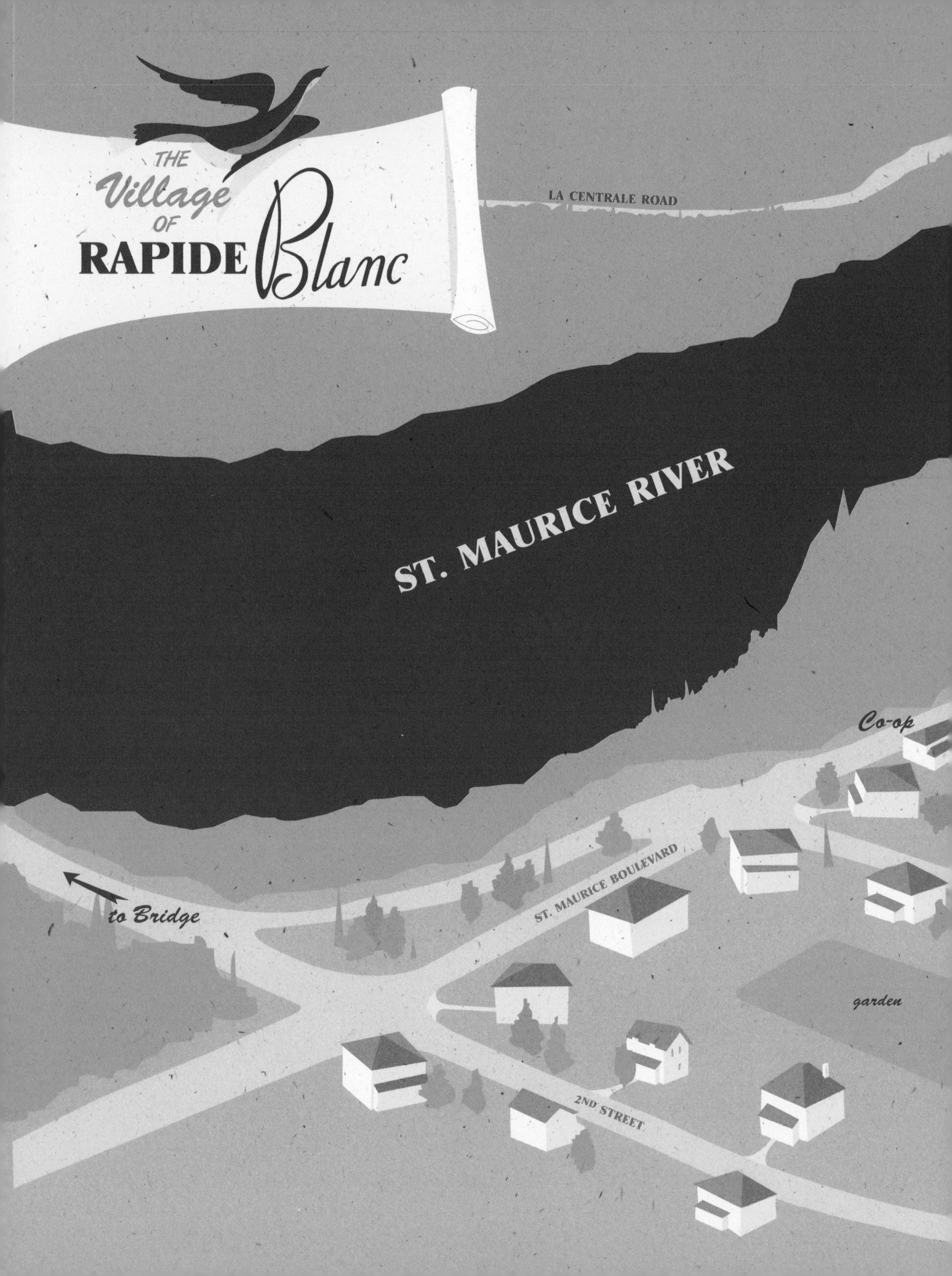
THE
Village
OF
RAPIDE Blanc
LA CENTRALE ROAD
ST. MAURICE RIVER
Co-op
to Bridge
ST. MAURICE BOULEVARD
garden
2ND STREET

Rapide Blanc
Power Plant & Dam
40 Ski hill
Staff House (Inn)
Anglican Church
Water Treatment
Plant
Tennis Court
CRESCENT STREET
Park
garden
ESCENT STREET
School
Curling
Club
1ST STREET
Garage
BOUTEILLE STREET
Catholic Churh
to Bouteille Creek

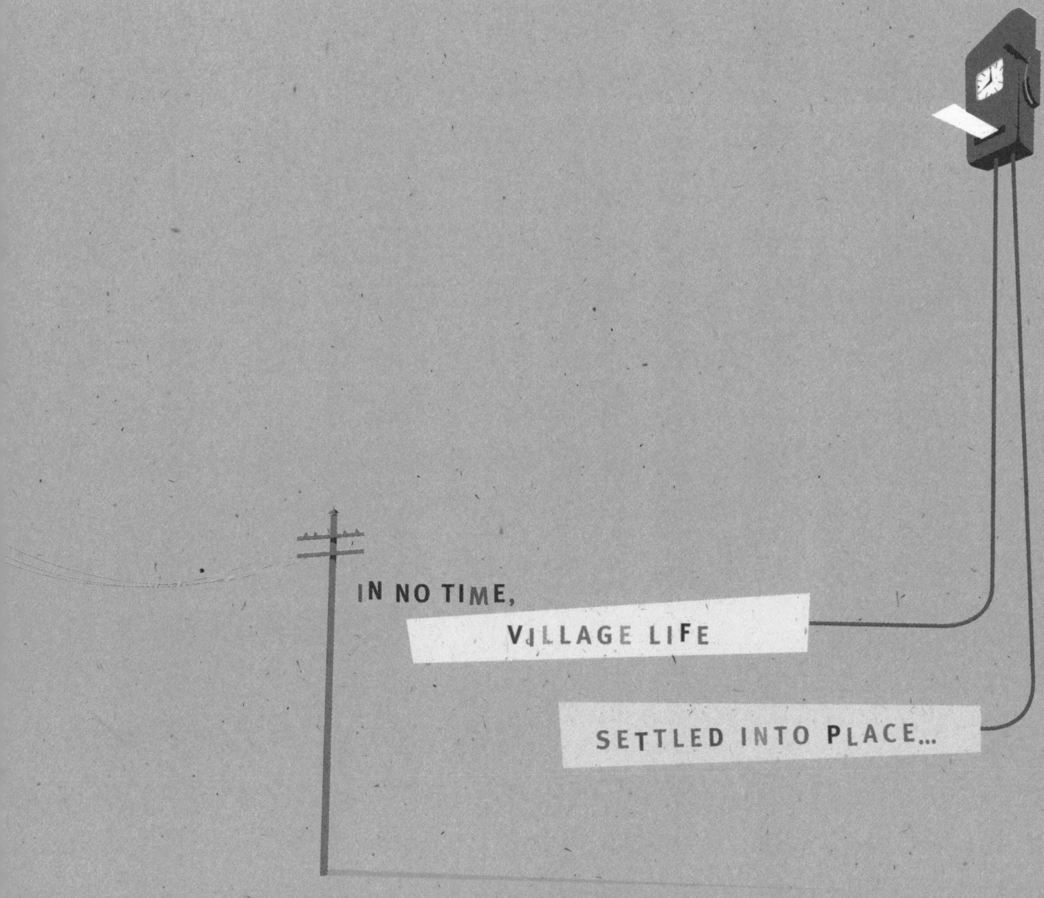

IN NO TIME,
VILLAGE LIFE
SETTLED INTO PLACE...

Kellogg's
CORN
FLAKES

At the Co-op, Conversation ranged from gossip to Baker's Chocolate to the bear hunt.
8
New flavor!
JELL-O
MINUTE RICE
PRE-COOKED
Makes PERFECT RICE Instantly
LONG-GRAIN WHITE

Ten miles out of town, the little Rapide Blanc railway station was the only link to civilization. You took the train to "go down to the city." The first car arrived by rail in 1935, and in just a few years, almost everybody had one.
The night train from La Tuque, the closest town south of Rapide Blanc, pulled in every day to deliver milk and mail, often bringing along the latest model refrigerator, a four-burner stove, a fashionable living room set or a brand new Chrysler.

Frank Spain ltd.
FURNITURE • APPLIANCES • RADIOS
LA TUQUE, QUEBEC

In the summer,
a shuttle bus drove back and forth
between Rapide Blanc and Croche Lake

SWP
VILLAGE TO BEACH IN TEN MINUTES!
THE ST. MAURICE TRANSPORT COMPANY: A DIVISION OF THE SHAWINIGAN WATER & POWER COMPANY

All it took was a diving board,
a slide and a floating dock,
and the company had a beach in place for the locals.
****

Some summer evenings, there was dancing in the village,
the gramophone playing under the stars,
laughter, small talk
and Mademoiselle Normand's bright eyes…

The End
Every week
a reel of
film came
up from La Tuque
Screenings cost 10¢
And so Rapide Blanc
laughed with Abbott and Costello,
shed a tear
to the goodbyes in Casablanca
and hummed Singin' in the Rain
on the way home
an M-G-M motion picture

School
Mary had a little lamb
Marie avait un mouton

1948

The baby boom called for a new school.
The population of Rapide Blanc
(240 inhabitants) was half French,
half English. One English class,
one French class. In the schoolyard,
the little Futter boy said "bondjiour"
instead of hello and the Bergeron
girl called her parents "fawder"
and "mawder" ...

Snow!
CRESCENT St.

On December 24th folks stayed up till midnight...

Merry
Christmas

Marconi

Winters in Rapide Blanc were severe.
Snowstorms buried the town and temperatures dropped to 50 degree Celsius below.
With all the lakes and rivers around, the cold was more biting than anywhere else...
It was during those never-ending winters
that the village's curling club hosted its legendary get-togethers...:

When Clovis
pulls out his fiddle,
you can bet the party
will go on all
night…

Come spring, snowmelt and strong rains swelled the waters of the St. Maurice, forcing the SW&P Co. to open the dam's floodgates. In the control room at the Rapide Blanc plant, operators waited for an OK from the head office in Shawinigan Falls.

4
5
6

hello?

Verdict:
OK guys!
open 'em up!

ALARM: ACTIVATE TO ENSURE
THAT MEN AND BOATS
MOVE AWAY FROM THE DAM.

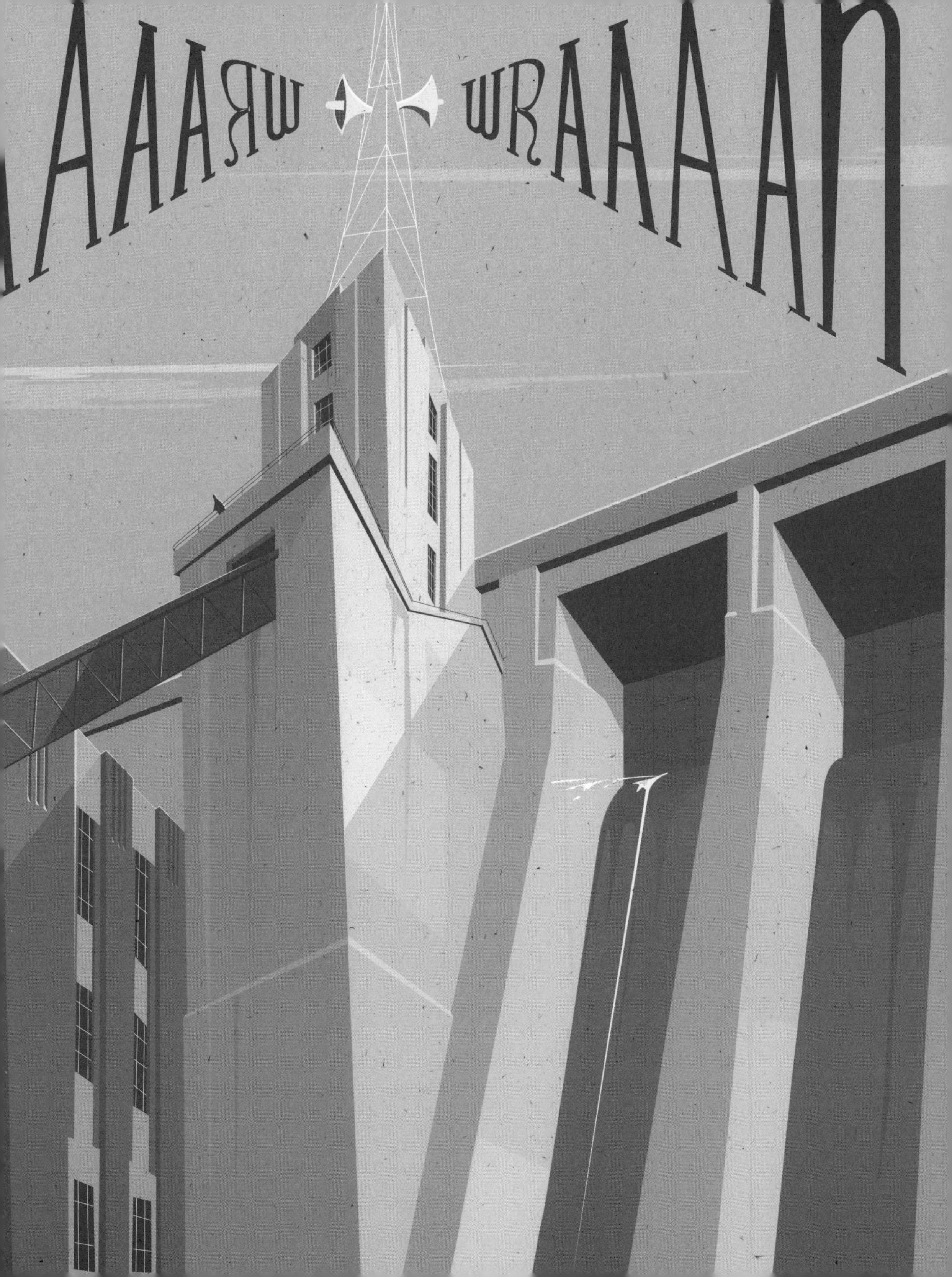
WRAAAAN

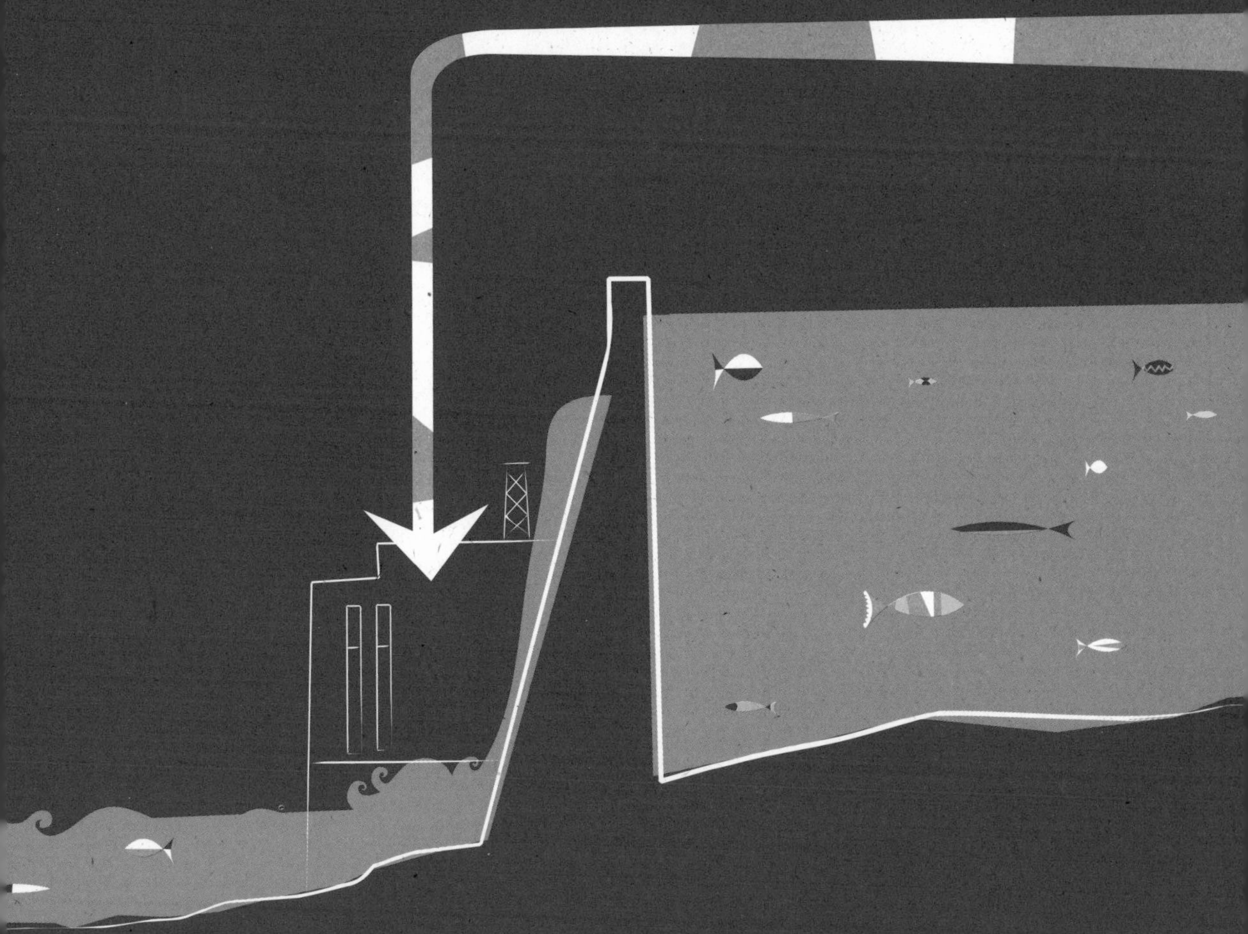

UPSTREAM OF THE DAM,
THE LOG DRIVE WOULD BE UNDERWAY,
BRINGING DRIVERS TO RAPIDE BLANC.
THE ST. MAURICE RIVER BOOM & DRIVING CO.
HANDLED THE FLOATING OF WOOD ALONG THE
ENTIRE 530 MILES OF THE RIVER,
DOWN TO THE PULP AND PAPER
MILLS IN SHAWINIGAN AND THREE RIVERS.
LOG DRIVERS WERE THE TRUE HEROES OF THE
MAURICIE REGION, AND THEY BROKE MORE
THAN A FEW HEARTS IN RAPIDE BLANC...

WEYMONTACHINGUE

GONE FISHING

The entire territory surrounding the village & dam belonged to the SW&P Co. With all the lakes nearby, the company turned this territory into a private fish and game club, strictly reserved for employees. Camps were built on the lakes, and it wasn't long before fishing became the No. 1 sport in Rapide Blanc.

WHEN THE OTTERS TURN UP, YOU MIGHT AS WELL TAKE A NAP...

NOTHING'S GONNA BITE...

UNDER THE VILLAGE
BRIDGE
LURKED
The
GENERAL

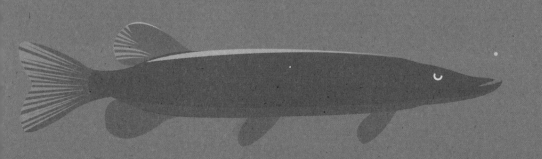

SOON EVERY FISHERMAN
IN TOWN HAD HIS EYES
ON THAT ENORMOUS PIKE.

FIERCELY AGGRESSIVE,
THE FISH WRECKED RODS
AND REELS AND CUT THROUGH LINES
WITH RAZOR-SHARP TEETH.

TALES OF FAILED ATTEMPTS TO CATCH
THE GENERAL MULTIPLIED,
AND BEFORE LONG,
YOU WOULD HAVE THOUGHT HE MEASURED
EIGHT ARM-LENGTHS...

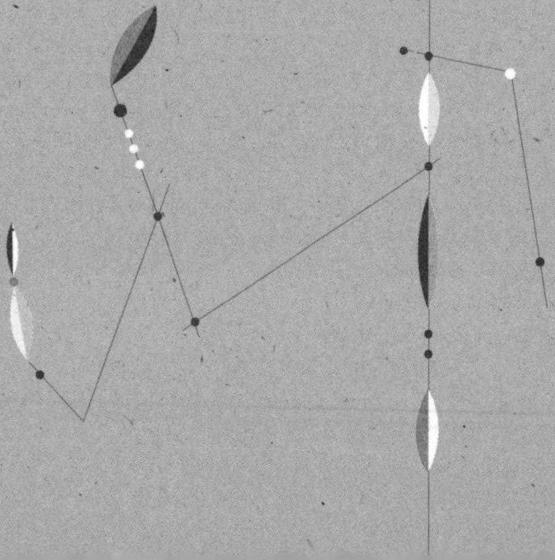

OVER THE YEARS,
THE GENERAL BECAME A LOCAL LEGEND...

SOME SAID THEY HAD SEEN HIM
PULL A DEER DRINKING BY THE RIVER'S EDGE
DOWN INTO ITS MURKY DEPTHS...

WHEN THE VILLAGE BRIDGE SHOOK,
OTHERS SAID IT WAS THE PIKE
PASSING THROUGH BELOW,
KNOCKING AGAINST THE PILINGS
BECAUSE HE WAS GOING BLIND...

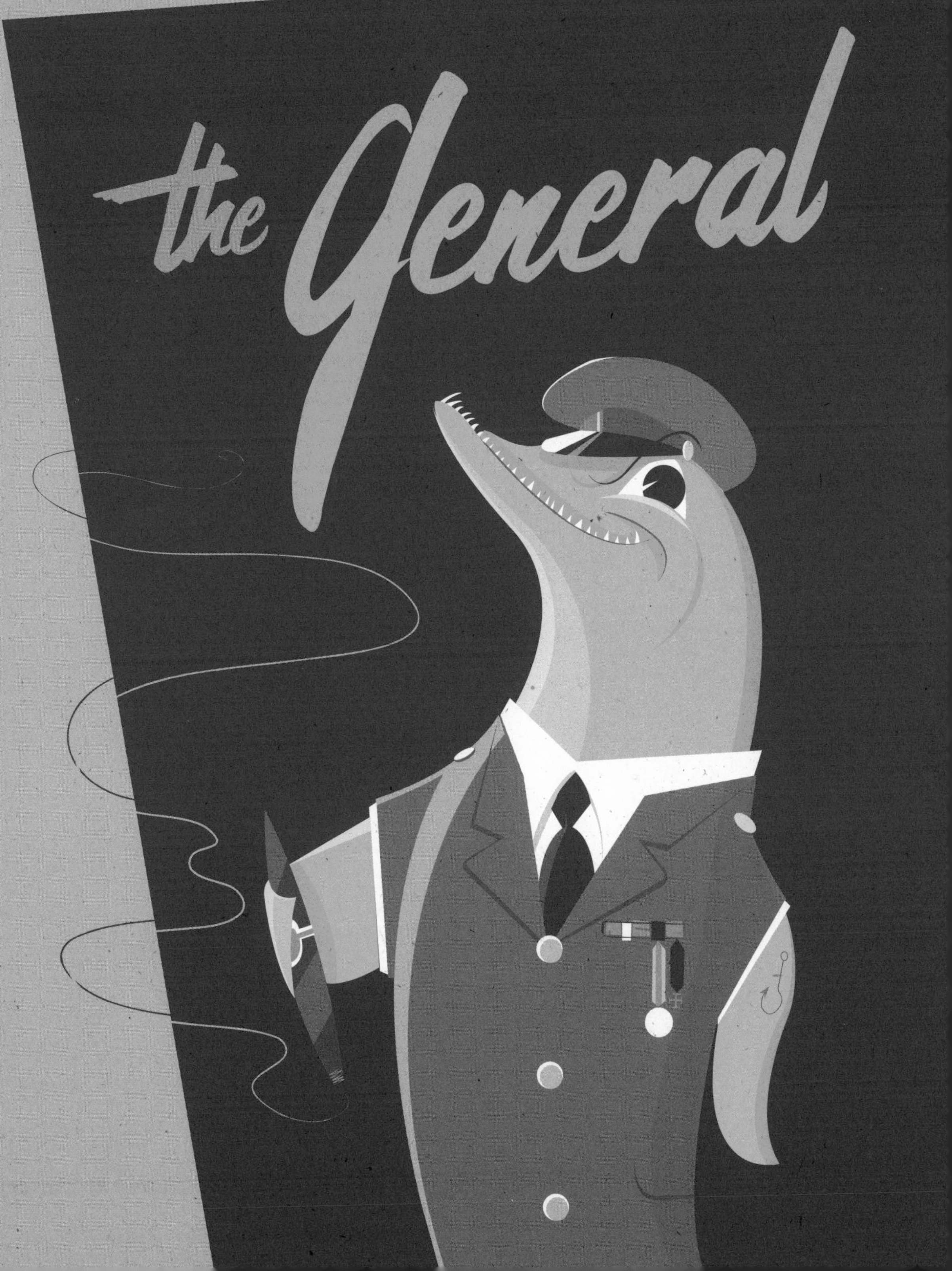
the General

MOOSE, PARTRIDGE,
BEAR, DEER
AND MANY MORE!
ONCE HUNTING
SEASON OPENS,
YOU CAN
FORGET
ABOUT FINDING
BIG LAWTON IN TOWN....

THE ROAD

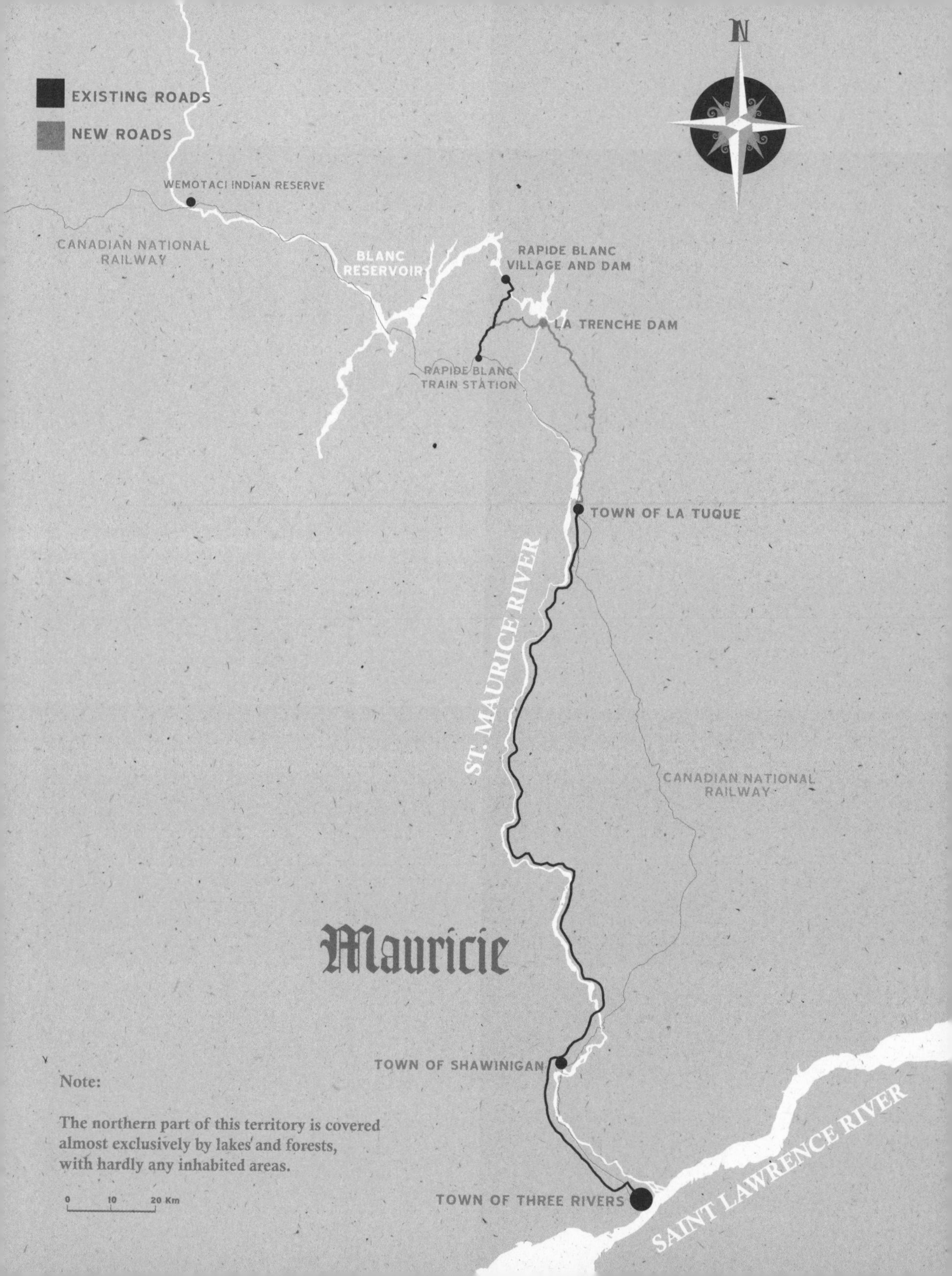
EXISTING ROADS
NEW ROADS
N
WEMOTACI INDIAN RESERVE
CANADIAN NATIONAL RAILWAY
BLANC RESERVOIR
RAPIDE BLANC VILLAGE AND DAM
LA TRENCHE DAM
RAPIDE BLANC TRAIN STATION
TOWN OF LA TUQUE
ST. MAURICE RIVER
CANADIAN NATIONAL RAILWAY
Mauricie
TOWN OF SHAWINIGAN
Note:
The northern part of this territory is covered almost exclusively by lakes and forests, with hardly any inhabited areas.
0 10 20 Km
TOWN OF THREE RIVERS
SAINT LAWRENCE RIVER

THE CONSTRUCTION OF THE MASSIVE LA TRENCHE DAM DOWNRIVER FROM RAPIDE BLANC USHERED IN A NEW ERA. A ROAD WOULD NOW CONNECT LA TUQUE TO LA TRENCHE AND LA TRENCHE TO RAPIDE BLANC.

VILLAGERS AND THEIR VISITORS COULD FINALLY ENJOY THE PLEASURES OF CAR TRAVEL...

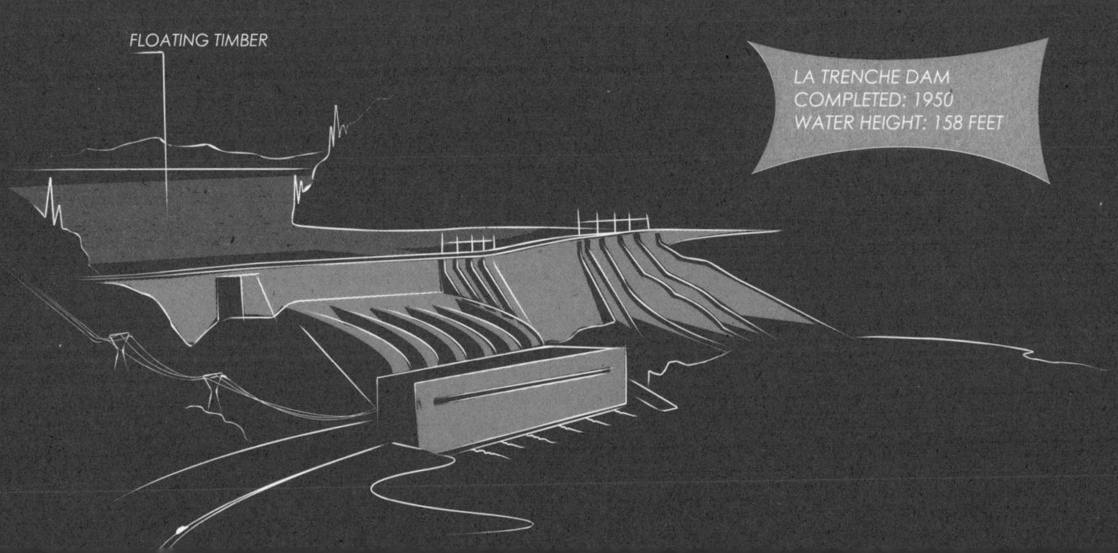

Braziiil, where hearts were entertaining June
We stood beneath an amber mooon
And softly murmured someday sooon…

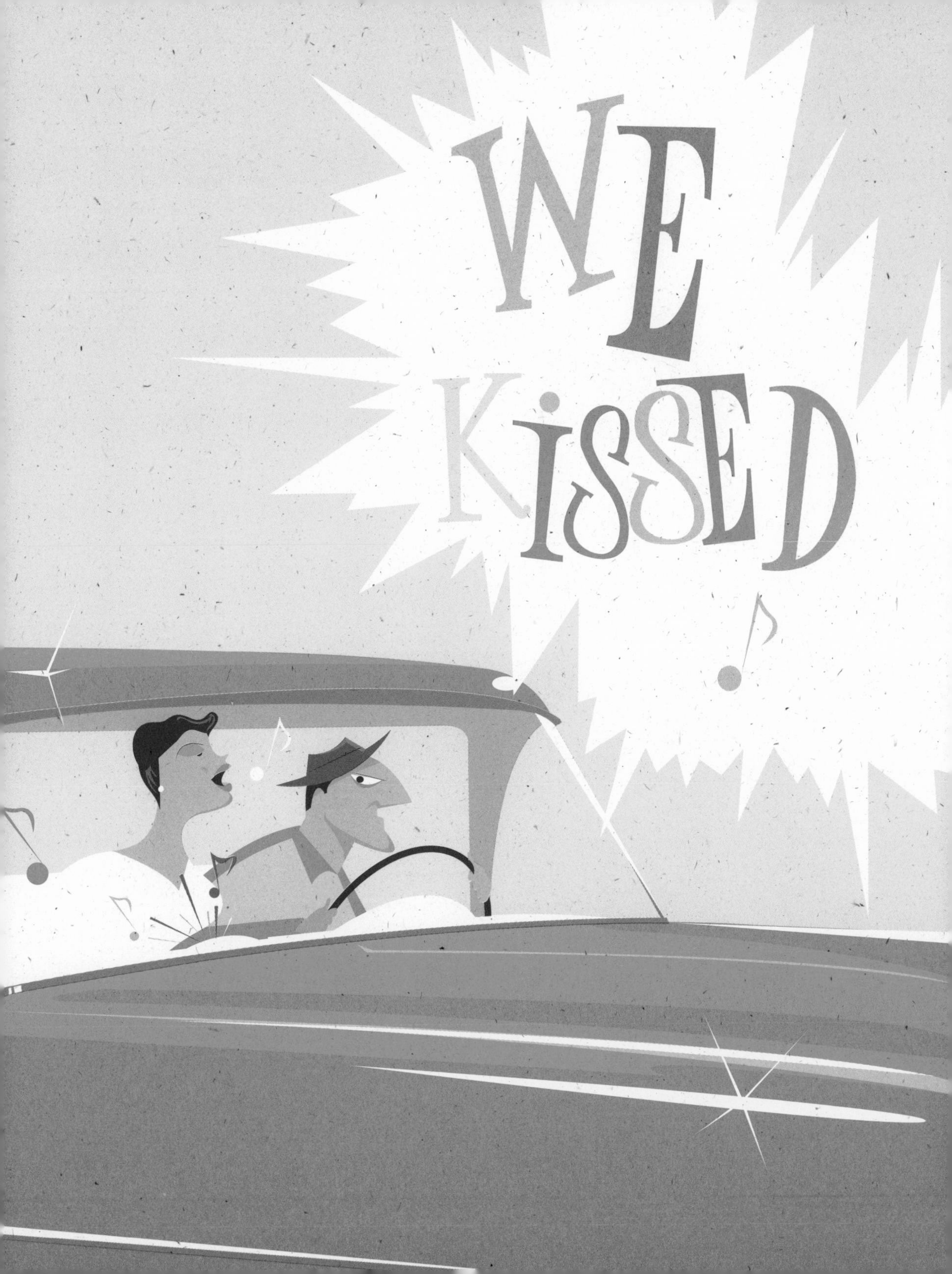
WE
KISSED

AND CLUNG
TO-GE-THER

The-e-en tomorrow was another daaay. . .

The morning found me miles awaaay...

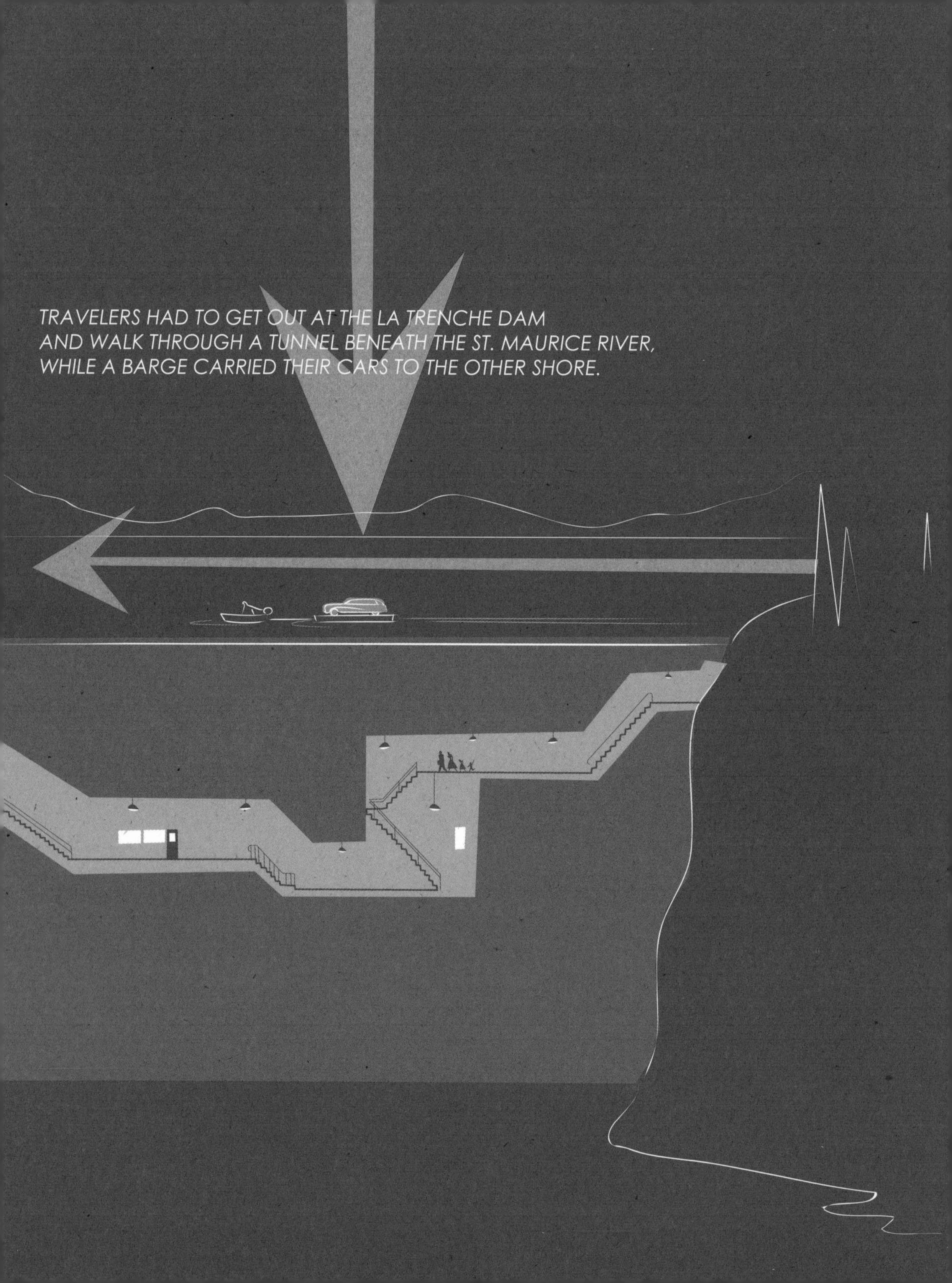
TRAVELERS HAD TO GET OUT AT THE LA TRENCHE DAM
AND WALK THROUGH A TUNNEL BENEATH THE ST. MAURICE RIVER,
WHILE A BARGE CARRIED THEIR CARS TO THE OTHER SHORE.

A few more miles, and you were in Rapide Blanc!

Years went by

MAINTENANT OU JAMAIS!

MAÎTRES CHEZ NOUS*

*NOW OR NEVER
MASTERS IN OUR OWN HOME

1963

NATIONALIZATION OF
THE ELECTRIC POWER
INDUSTRY IN QUEBEC .
THE PROVINCIAL GOVERNMENT
BOUGHT OUT ALL PRIVATE ELECTRICITY
COMPANIES TO CREATE HYDRO QUÉBEC.
THE SHAWINIGAN WATER AND
POWER COMPANY WAS DISSOLVED.
THE HEADQUARTERS OF
THE YOUNG GOVERNMENT
CORPORATION WERE BUILT AT
75 DORCHESTER BOULEVARD
IN MONTREAL.
A LONG WAY AWAY,
IN RAPIDE BLANC,
A RUMOR BEGAN TO SPREAD...

WHAT?
YOU'RE KIDDI

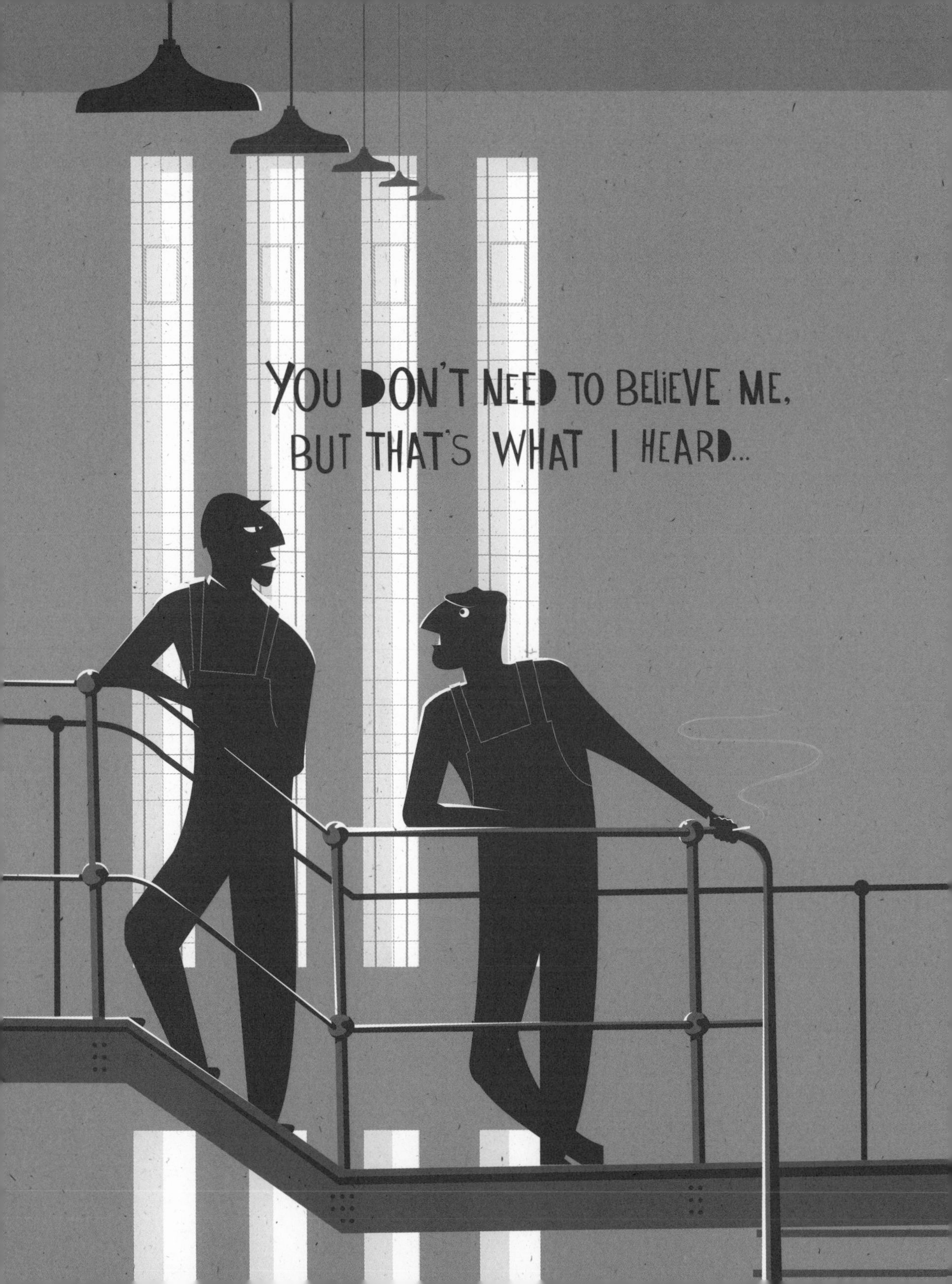
YOU DON'T NEED TO BELIEVE ME,
BUT THAT'S WHAT I HEARD...

AND THEN ONE MORNING, FROM HIS FRONT PORCH,
THE SUPERINTENDENT PUT AN END TO THE RUMORS...
HIS STATEMENT WAS SHORT AND UNEQUIVOCAL

is it true?
who decided?
everyone's leaving?
when?
I knew it ...
will we be transferred?
so it's true after all....
how soon?
did you speak with them?
c'mon, germaine!
what did they say?
I told you so...
you mean...of course!
what?
and what about the power plant?
how will it run?
really? oh...
jeezus...
who said so?
that's progress for you...
i don't care, i still think it's crazy!
crazy or not, we don't really have a choice
and what about us?
back south, I guess...
gérard says he knew...
since when?
that long?
but Leo, this is our home...

?

SORRY GUYS...

Automation Marches On

CLOSURE OF THE TOWN OF RAPIDE BLANC

The Hydro-Québec Commission has authorized the automation of the Rapide Blanc and La Trenche power plants and their remote monitoring via the La Tuque generating station.

The company's management has also decided to build a microwave communications network to connect the Rapide Blanc and La Trenche power plants to the power plant in La Tuque. From there, the network will be extended to Mont Carmel, where it will be integrated into Hydro-Québec's provincial communications network.

Estimated at $2.5 million, the implementation of the two projects will result in the closure of the Town of Rapide Blanc, as well as the transfer of 71 employees currently operating and maintaining the dams. Some 54 families, or a total of 240 people, will be affected by the transfers.

These significant changes should be completed by the summer of 1971.

MANPOWER

As early as July 1969, all permanent employees of the Town of Rapide Blanc will be advised of the new positions to which they will be assigned in the summer of 1971. The Human Resources Service of the Center Zone, based in Shawinigan, will begin consultations on February 3 to involve all individuals in selecting their future employment.

AUTOMATION

There are four major reasons for Hydro-Québec's decision to automate the Rapide Blanc and La Trenche power plants and close down the village.

First is the continuous improvement of communication networks and road transportation. Today, one can easily drive from Shawinigan to Rapide Blanc, hold a meeting and drive back all in the same day. When the village was founded in 1928, travel from Shawinigan to Rapide Blanc was a major expedition.

Second, improvements in the standard of living in Quebec mean that employees, regardless of their position, want to work near commercial centers, schools and hospitals. In other words, they want access to urban facilities.

In a town like Rapide Blanc, providing residents with all the comforts of modern living is simply not financially viable.

Furthermore, Hydro-Québec must take into account certain economic considerations. The automation of the Rapide Blanc and La Trenche dams plus the closure of the town will generate annual savings estimated at $450,000. Accordingly, the capital investment, estimated at $2.5 million, should be recovered in less than six years. As such, the investment is entirely consistent with the requirements of sound and dynamic management.

Lastly, a human resources survey conducted by the utility's Organization and Methods Service recorded 115 changes in positions in the Center Zone in 1968 (retirement, transfer, promotion, resignation, etc.). The company is confident that employees affected by the closure of the Town of Rapide Blanc will view their reassignment in a positive light. It should be noted that the movement of personnel is conditioned to an extent by current collective agreements within the company.

Thus, employees are guaranteed new positions with no loss of salary. Robert A. Boyd, speaking in Rouyn after the closure of the Village of Rapide VII in Abitibi East, referred to this policy when he said, "The automation of the Hydro-Québec network cannot proceed more quickly than the prudent and rational reassignment of the company's EMPLOYEES." In early February, a draft outline of the future organizational structures of the Upper St. Maurice complex will be submitted for approval to Hydro-Québec management. This preliminary study will guide the reassignment of employees affected by the closure.

THE FATE OF THE TOWN

As for the Town and the Fish and Game Club, the Center Zone has been assigned to negotiate future uses with the Department of Tourism, Fish and Game. The Department is responsible for making public the outcome of these negotiations.

With the automation of the Rapide Blanc and La Trenche power plants and the closure of the Town, Hydro-Québec is committing itself to a technical and human resources project of considerable scale. The company intends to make it a success, in the best interest of both its employees and its customers.

1971

From now on, the train would no longer stop at the Rapide Blanc station. The priest would stop coming and the pleasant murmur of summer evenings would be silenced forever.

MOV

Why are you stopping?
Hold on, I'll only be a minute...

PLOP!

195 CRESCENT

The General WAS NEVER CAUGHT.

The end
RAPIDE BLANC →

Discography

RAPIDE

SCENE	TITLE	ARTIST	DATE
OUVERTURE	GERSHWIN, PIANO CONCERTO IN F	ANDRÉ PREVIN & THE LONDON SYMPHONY ORCH.	1925 REC: 1971
ALL ABOARD!	FIVE FOOT TWO, EYES OF BLUE	THE SAVOY ORPHEANS	1926
CONSTRUCTION OF THE VILLAGE	MARINELLA	TINO ROSSI	1936
THE SHIFT	'TAIN'T WHAT YOU DO	JIMMIE LUNCEFORD and His ORCHESTRA	1939
THE CO-OP	YOU ARE MY SUNSHINE	BING CROSBY	1941
RAPIDE BLANC STATION	OPUS ONE	TOMMY DORSEY and His ORCHESTRA	1944
THE BEACH	RUM AND COCA-COLA	THE ANDREWS SISTERS	1944
SUMMER NIGHTS	STARDUST	ARTIE SHAW and His ORCHESTRA	1949
THE MOVIES	SINGIN' IN THE RAIN	THE M-G-M STUDIO ORCHESTRA	1951
SCHOOL	"A" YOU'RE ADORABLE	GORDON MACRAE and JO STAFFORD	1949
SNOW!	SH-BOOM	THE CREW-CUTS	1953
MERRY CHRISTMAS	MELE KALIKIMAKA	BING CROSBY and The ANDREWS SISTERS	1950
THE CURLING CLUB	LE RAPIDE BLANC	OSCAR THIFAULT et LES AS DE LA GAMME	1955

D R A W N & Q U A R T E R L Y

BLANC

SCENE	TITLE	ARTIST	DATE
THE FLOOD GATES	POWER HOUSE	AMBROSE and His ORCHESTRA	1930s
GONE FISHING	GONE FISHIN'	BING CROSBY and LOUIS ARMSTRONG	1951
THE GENERAL	SINGING THE BLUES	GUY MITCHELL	1956
ON THE ROAD	BRAZIL	BING CROSBY & ROSEMARY CLOONEY	1958
NATIONALIZATION	THE LION SLEEPS TONIGHT	THE TOKENS	1962
THE RUMOR	TOM DOOLEY	LES COMPAGNONS DE LA CHANSON	1959
1971	THIS IS HEAVEN TO ME	MADELEINE PEYROUX	2004
THE END	GENTLE ON MY MIND	DEAN MARTIN	1969

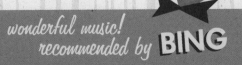

wonderful music!
recommended by **BING**

A BOUT THE AUTHOR

Pascal Blanchet

was born in Trois-Rivières, formerly also known as Three Rivers, in 1980.

His interests include 20th century design, architecture and jazz.

His work can be found on the covers of Penguin Books and in the pages of The San Francisco Magazine and The New Yorker.

His first book, La Fugue, was published by La Pastèque in 2005 to popular and critical acclaim, winning the 2005 Bédélys Award for best Québec comic book of the year.

WWW.PASCALBLANCHET.CA